---

*This book was a gift
to our library
from Capstone Press.*

Grasslands

by Sally Wilkins

Consultant:
Francesca Pozzi, Research Associate
Center for International Earth Science Information Network
Columbia University

Bridgestone Books
an imprint of Capstone Press
Mankato, Minnesota

Bridgestone Books are published by Capstone Press
151 Good Counsel Drive, P.O. Box 669, Mankato, Minnesota 56002
http://www.capstone-press.com

Library of Congress Cataloging-in-Publication Data
Wilkins, Sally.
  Grasslands/by Sally Wilkins.
  p. cm.—(The Bridgestone science library)
  Includes bibliographical references and index.
  ISBN 0-7368-0837-X
  1. Grasslands—Juvenile literature. [1. Grasslands.] I. Title. II. Series.
QH87.7 .W55 2001
578.74—dc21   00-009917

Summary: Discusses the plants, animals, and climate in grassland ecosystems.

Editorial Credits
Karen L. Daas, editor; Karen Risch, product planning editor; Linda Clavel, designer and
    illustrator; Heidi Schoof, photo researcher

Photo Credits
Corel, 5, 7, 9, 11, 13, 15, 17, 19, 21
Doug Sokell/Tom Stack & Associates, 8
Inga Spence/Tom Stack & Associates, 18
James P. Rowan, 6, 10, 12, 14
Root Resources/Mary M. Tremaine, cover, 1
Shaffer Photography/James L. Shaffer, 20
Victoria Hurst/Tom Stack & Associates, 16

Table of Contents

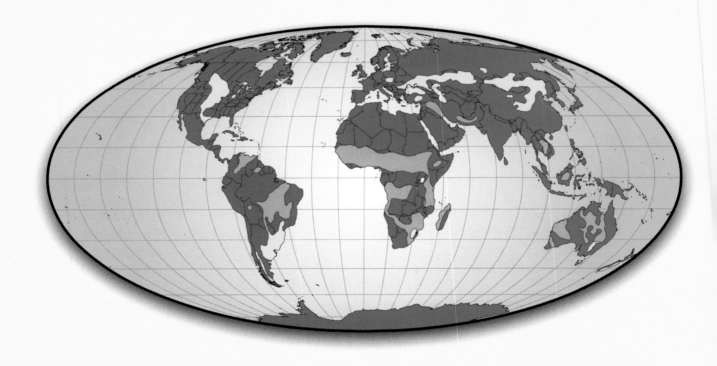

temperate grasslands
tropical grasslands (savannas)

Grassland Facts

- Grasslands cover about one-fourth of Earth's land. This area is about 14 million square miles (36 million square kilometers).

- Grasslands grow on every continent except Antarctica. Tropical grasslands grow near the equator.

- Temperate grasslands receive 10 to 30 inches (25 to 76 centimeters) of rain each year. Tropical grasslands receive 25 to 60 inches (64 to 152 centimeters) of rain each year.

- Grasslands are grouped by the average height of their grasses. Tall grasslands grow to be about 5 feet (1.5 meters) high. Mixed grasslands are 2 to 3 feet (.6 to .9 meters) high. Short grasslands have very short grasses. These areas look like deserts.

- Most of the world's food comes from grasslands. Wheat and corn are grasses.

Grasslands

Grasslands receive more rain than deserts and less rain than forests. Many kinds of grasses cover grasslands. Some small trees and shrubs also grow in grasslands.

Grasslands have temperate or tropical climates. North American prairies are temperate grasslands. They are warm in the summer and cool in the winter. Savannas are tropical grasslands. South America, Africa, Asia, and Australia have savannas. Temperatures in the savannas stay about the same all year.

Grasslands have wet seasons and dry seasons. Temperate grasslands usually receive between 10 and 30 inches (25 and 76 centimeters) of rain each year. Most of the rain falls in late spring and early summer. Tropical grasslands receive 25 to 60 inches (64 to 152 centimeters) of rain each winter. A long dry season follows the wet season. Grasses become so dry that they burn easily.

Grasslands grow near the Badlands in South Dakota.

Grassland Soil

More than 8,000 types of grasses grow in grasslands. The types of grasses that grow in an area depend on the soil and climate.

Grassland soil has several layers. The top layer is humus. Rotted animals and plants make up this fertile level.

Topsoil is the second layer. Rain and heat soak minerals from the humus into the topsoil. Grasses and plants often take root in the topsoil.

Subsoil lies below the topsoil. The subsoil stores water during wet seasons. The water rises to the topsoil during dry seasons. Grasses and plants in the topsoil then absorb the water through their roots. The subsoil in tropical climates is deeper than it is in temperate climates. Rain and heat move matter from the humus and topsoil into the subsoil.

All grasslands have humus, topsoil, and subsoil. Some grasslands also have a layer of solid rock below these layers.

Rich humus forms the top layer of soil in a grassland.

Animals in the Grasslands

Prairie dogs live in North American grasslands. These rodents dig many underground burrows. These tunnels connect to form a prairie dog town. A prairie dog town can cover more than 160 acres (65 hectares).

Millions of bison once roamed North American prairies. Hunters killed these large animals for food and for sport. Today, about 65,000 bison live in North America.

Kangaroos make their homes in Australian grasslands. Kangaroos are marsupials. This type of animal carries its young in a pouch on its body.

African savannas are home to many animals. Elephants, giraffes, and zebras live there. Lions and rhinos also make their homes in savannas.

Many birds live in grasslands around the world. Hawks, owls, and sparrows are common in North American grasslands. Bustards make their homes in African and Asian grasslands.

Prairie dogs dig prairie dog towns. These underground burrows can cover more than 160 acres (65 hectares).

Plants in the Grasslands

Grasses are the most common plants in a grassland. Grasses grow almost everywhere in the world.

Grasses can be annuals or perennials. Annual grasses live for about one year. They grow quickly in the spring. Annual grasses die when they run out of food and water in the fall. Perennial grasses live for several years. They store food in their roots for cold or dry times.

Sunflowers, chicory, and corn marigolds grow on temperate grasslands. In the past, many other colorful wildflowers also grew on temperate grasslands. Today, farmers use chemicals on their crops. The plants cannot grow in the new soil. The soil no longer has the nutrients the plants need.

People plant crops in cultivated grasslands. They remove the top layer of the grassland to prepare the soil for crops. Farmers plant corn, wheat, rye, oats, and barley in fields. These plants grow well in the rich soil.

Prairie coneflowers grow on prairies. These plants grow to be about 2 feet (61 centimeters) tall.

The Grassland Ecosystem

The plants and animals in a grassland are part of an ecosystem. The climate and soil also make up the grassland ecosystem.

The grasses depend on the soil in a grassland. Grasses cannot grow without nutrients and water from the soil.

The plants and animals in the grasslands also depend on each other. They form a food chain. The plants make their own food using nutrients from the soil and energy from the sun. Small animals eat the plants. Larger animals then eat the smaller animals. Animals rot after they die and add nutrients to the soil. The nutrients then become food for plants, including grasses.

Fire has an important role in a grassland ecosystem. Fires may start when lightning strikes dry grasslands. The dry grasses burn. But roots remain unharmed. They produce new grasses at the start of the wet season.

Zebras living on the savanna eat grasses.

The Serengeti

The Serengeti is a grassland in eastern Africa. Serengeti means "endless plain." The Maasai, a group of native people in Africa, gave the grassland this name. The Serengeti covers 15,000 square miles (38,850 square kilometers) in Tanzania and Kenya.

The Serengeti has different types of grasslands. Open, grassy plains grow in the south. The central and eastern regions are savannas. Savannas receive less rain than the open plains. Wooded grasslands cover the northern area. Black clay plains form the western border of the Serengeti. Rivers, lakes, and swamps lie in several areas of the Serengeti.

More than 3 million animals live in the Serengeti. Elephants, giraffes, and zebras make their home in the Serengeti during wet seasons. They eat newly grown grass. They then travel to other areas to search for food and water during dry seasons.

Yellow-barked Acacia trees grow in the northern area of the Serengeti.

17

Grassland Resources

A grassland's most valuable resource is its fertile soil. Farmers around the world plant crops in grassland soil. The crops help feed millions of people each year.

Farmers graze cattle and sheep on grasslands. Many people eat meat from cattle. People make clothes from sheep wool.

In the past, people hunted animals that live in native grasslands. They tracked and killed antelope and bison across North American prairies. In Africa, hunters went on safaris. They tracked and killed lions, elephants, and leopards. Many kinds of animals began to disappear. Today, governments protect native grassland animals. People no longer can hunt these animals.

Scientists travel to natural grasslands to learn more about grassland ecosystems. They study the roles of fire and water in grasslands. They try to discover better ways to use and protect grasslands.

Farmers plant wheat in fertile grassland soil.

Changing Grasslands

Cultivated grasslands are replacing natural grasslands. Farmers break up grasslands when they plow soil to plant crops. The crops take nutrients from the soil. Farmers then harvest the crops when they are ripe.

Farmers often pump water from the subsoil to the surface. Crops need more water than grasses do to grow. Grasslands then dry out during the dry season. The area does not have enough water stored in the subsoil for plants to live. The topsoil is not protected from the hot sun. The grassland areas can become deserts.

Farm animals graze on grasslands. The grasses that animals eat may not grow back quickly. The wind blows topsoil away. Dirt covers the land.

People sometimes plant grass seed on old farmland. They hope to keep a balance between natural and cultivated grasslands.

Farm animals such as cows graze on grassland grasses.

Hands On: Grow Grass

Some seeds grow more quickly than other seeds. You can compare how quickly seeds grow.

What You Need

Grass seeds
Two kinds of plant seeds
Three small flower pots filled with soil
Water
Ruler

What You Do

1. Plant grass seeds in a flower pot.
2. Plant one plant seed into each remaining flower pot.
3. Place the plants in the sun.
4. Water the seeds each day for two weeks.
5. Measure how tall the grass and plants grow.

Grasses usually grow faster than plants. They quickly cover grassland soil and protect it from the wind.

Words to Know

burrow (BUR-oh)—a tunnel in the ground dug by animals
climate (KLYE-mit)—the usual weather in a place
drought (DROUT)—a long period of time without rainfall
ecosystem (EE-koh-siss-tuhm)—a community of plants and animals interacting with their environment
fertile (FUR-tuhl)—having many nutrients
humus (HYOO-muhss)—a rich, nutrient-filled layer of soil
marsupial (mar-SOO-pee-uhl)—a type of animal that carries its young in a pouch on its body
nutrient (NOO-tree-uhnt)—something that is needed by animals and plants to stay healthy
perennial (puh-REN-ee-uhl)—a plant that lives for more than two years
safari (suh-FAH-ree)—a trip to see or hunt large animals

Read More

Behar, Susie. *Grasslands.* Brookfield, Conn.: Copper Beech Books, 2000.

Savage, Stephen. *Animals of the Grasslands.* Animals by Habitat. Austin, Texas: Raintree Steck-Vaughn, 1997.

Stille, Darlene R. *Grasslands.* A True Book. New York: Children's Press, 1999.

Useful Addresses

Canadian Wildlife Federation
350 Michael Cowpland Drive
Kanata, ON K2M 2W1
Canada

The Nature Conservancy
1815 North Lynn Street
Arlington, VA 22209

Internet Sites

Canterbury Environmental Education Centre
http://www.naturegrid.org.uk/children.html
Grasslands Biome
http://mbgnet.mobot.org/pfg/diverse/biomes/grasslnd/
  index.htm
What's it Like Where You Live?
http://mbgnet.mobot.org/sets/grasslnd/index.htm

Index